BINGES & BALANCE BEAMS

My Secret Search for Myself

Nutrition, Gymnastics and Fitness Expert

BETSY MCNALLY-LAOUAR

BETSY MCNALLY

DISCLAIMER:

The sole purpose of this book is to educate and inspire. There is no guarantee made by the author or the publisher that anyone following the ideas, tips, suggestions, techniques, or strategies will become successful. The author and publisher shall have neither liability nor responsibility to anyone with respect to any loss or damage caused, or alleged to be caused, directly or indirectly by the information contained in this book.

*This book is dedicated to my sons,
Lenny and Ayden.*

*May they one day know the challenges of their
mother and how much I love them.*

CONTENTS

FOREWORD

WE LIVE IN A WORLD of extremes. We see our culture fueled by the excitement of extreme sports and entertained by the twenty-plus reality shows with the word "extreme" in the title.

In today's world, there is a tremendous amount of pressure to be extreme. So, many of us strive to be the best, richest, fastest, most successful, prettiest, and, of course, to have the perfect body. You probably picked up this book because you can relate to the roller coaster life of extremes. I know I can.

I, too, come from a gymnastics background and was plagued by the elusive thrill of victory as I monitored every morsel I put into my mouth. I also struggled with binge eating and restricting. There were times I felt on top of the world when eating "perfect," only to fall into intense self-loathing when eating "crap."

Both in my own gymnastics career and in my current work as a mental toughness coach for athletes, over the last twenty-five years, I have seen so many athletes struggle with the cycle of extremes. I've encountered the struggle both in terms of their relationship with food as well as the mental anguish over never feeling quite good enough.

But this pattern is not only in athletes. It exists in all walks of life, from the mom to the manager, which is one reason why this book is so important. We all have dealt with this type of pressure on some level.

I met Betsy at Cincinnati Gymnastics in the fall of 2009. I didn't realize she was in the middle of her own struggles with bingeing and self-acceptance at that time. I found her open, extremely knowledgeable, and willing to help anyone in need. In the years to come, we would develop a closer friendship, ultimately working together in our Tight Mind-Tight Body Boot Camps online.

I'm always amazed at how people respond to Betsy and the information she provides about nutrition and balance during our boot camps. She changes people's lives. Not only the athlete's life but their entire family's, as well! The people participating in our boot camps make huge changes. They learn for the first time about clean, healthy eating, and how to make it a part of their lives. They also learn about self-acceptance and discover tools to calm their body-image demons. It's so important these young athletes learn these tools now. I have seen many people find long-sought-after peace within Betsy's teachings.

One of the most impactful things I've witnessed in our boot camps is Betsy's candor in sharing about her own journey. She is willing to put herself out there, in order to facilitate change in others. When she shares about her experiences with food and perfection, we access that dark place that lives in many of us. We go on the journey with her, learn from her mistakes, develop self-compassion, and, hopefully, come out a little closer to that light at the end of the tunnel.

There are so many of us who need to find peace with body image and food. This book helps us do that. In a simple, brave, and honest format, Betsy talks about dark places that many of us know too well. She describes with candor ways of thinking and behaving we can all identify with. That is the beauty of this book. It is a lighthouse, a path to follow, and Betsy is our guide.

In a time when so many of us compare, compete, and worry about external attributes, this book helps us go inside, face our demons, and subsequently find the blessing of it all. I hope this book brings hope, peace, and self-acceptance to those that struggle. Our relationship with ourselves and our bodies is journey and with proper insight, we might even call it an adventure. It brings me joy to think that, through this book, we journey together.

Alison Arnold Ph.D.

Founder, HeadGames Mental Toughness
www.headgamesworld.com

INTRODUCTION

YOU ARE PROBABLY reading this book because the title and subject matter touch you. Maybe you are in the thick of this issue right now or know someone who is. Food addiction is real. It is like any other addiction: alcohol, drugs, etc. The problem with the addiction to food, however, is that it is legal and so very accessible. In order to live, you have to eat! So it's an addiction that stares you in the face every day and never goes away.

This book was painful to write. I did not enjoy doing it, but I did so because I want to help people. The process will have been worthwhile if I can help someone, even just one person, change their belief that binge eating is a disease they will have to live with for the rest of their life.

I didn't enjoy going through every detail of my obsessive and compulsive behavior with food and exercise in order to share my story with you. I don't like recounting my deepest past issues and insecurities. I feel the shame all over again that I've felt for many years when I recount this dirty, horrible secret I have kept to myself from so many.

Let me tell you this: there will be some disturbing accounts of my crazy binges. Believe me, I had serious issues, and I have had to overcome a lot to find balance in my life. I am allowing myself to be extremely vulnerable, in order to help someone or to help many who are struggling and have nowhere to turn or who may think no one understands.

This is the story of how a normal, healthy, well-adjusted woman could go from being fit and well to being an obsessive food and exercise addict. It's my personal journey of going from extremely fit to extremely fat. It describes my struggle with being out of control, out of balance, and depressed, searching for self-worth. I share my deep looking within and the ways I eventually overcame this disease. I'm here to tell about the despair and also to give hope, all through one woman's story. I want this book to show everyone *it can be done*.

As I describe my journey from being a regular fitness girl to an obsessed, addicted, and fat out-of-shape girl, you'll experience my story of binge eating, obsessive exercising, and recovery.

Yes, I *have* in fact fully recovered from my binge-eating disorder and exercise bulimia (where I tried to out-exercise a bad diet). It took time, years, and patience. It took years of reading, self-study, deep soul-searching, and even moving to another country, going through a divorce, remarrying, and having children in my late thirties and early forties. It's a story many women will be able to relate to. I know they will understand and find hope within it.

This is the story of a woman who has struggled in life but overcome. Of a woman who wants to live to help her autistic son and be healthy for both her children and her family. It's about a woman who wants to inspire and be a hero to people who have struggled like her....

If you are a compulsive eater, an ex-athlete, ex-bodybuilder, fitness competitor, or ex-gymnast, binge eater or anorexic or obsessive exerciser, this book will speak to you. It will give you hope. It will make you understand that you are not alone. And it will help you see that there are second, third, and fourth chances to beat addiction.

This is my story... My personal but universal search for balance and the happy ending of how I finally did realize it.

GROWING UP AN ATHLETE

THE WOMEN PORTRAYED in fitness magazines have perfect bodies, tanned perfect skin, and toned full muscles. They don't have an ounce of fat on their bodies. Nothing but healthy living could lead to this: a good diet, lots of exercise, and a healthy lifestyle.

This could be you, right?

Well, it was me. I am an IFBB PRO in fitness. I lived this life and looked like that. For a while, yes, I was doing it the right way, through balanced calories, running, and weight training. But over a period of time, this fit look became an obsession, something I couldn't control. I was always striving for more fitness, more strength, something better...

But why? And for whom? Why did I want to be so ultimately fit? Who was I trying to impress? In order to answer these questions, I had to dig deep, and when I did, I uncovered many truths about myself, about the fitness industry, the world of gymnastics, and about all of the very impossible expectations put on women in our culture to be perfect, fit, and flawless.

Let me say something about fitness models and competitors. Many of them are not the walking image of health that you think they are. Some may have eating disorders or may be obsessive exercisers, being extreme with cardio, severely restricting their diets, binging, or they may be a combination of any or all of these.

I'm not suggesting that every single woman who has ever been a fitness model, fitness competitor, or bodybuilder has had an eating disorder. But let's look at the facts.

Most of these women have extreme personalities. In order to have a super-physique that is fit, you need to really restrict and watch calories and do a lot of cardio, clean eating, and weight training. Unless you are one-hundred-percent blessed genetically, in order to do this alone, most of these women need to have an extremely disciplined lifestyle. The problem is that these women are our ideals. If we have a Type-A personality, that perfect body is something we will always be striving for.

How do I know this? I know this because I lived it. I was one of those extremely fit women whom you would see in a fitness magazine or walking on stage at a fitness show. I did this for a decade.

My food restricting caused a pattern of behavior that most obese people struggle with in their own food addictions and yo-yo diets. Of course, when I was dieting I would feel great: lean, super-energetic, and attractive. I would have lots of confidence and feel on top of the world...

But the second I would slip and have a bite of cake, a piece of bread, or God forbid some pasta, my blood sugar would skyrocket, and the desire to eat and eat and eat became uncontrollable. Since

I'd already screwed up, I would continue to eat badly, then even worse, to the point of becoming sick.

I have always been one of these Type-A perfectionists: a goal-setter, a risk-taker, someone inspired to do what someone else told me I couldn't do. While this is a good character trait, it is also a double-edged sword, as it can lead to obsessive-compulsive behavior and unrealistic self-expectations. This issue is complex, deep, and has taken me years to unravel.

You see, I was raised in the home of an NFL coach. When your dad is a coach for an NFL team, you understand and know the pressures of sport. You get that performance, dedication, and hard work pay off with glory, championships, and money. You see the hard work and the day-in-day-out grind of the professional sports world. I grew up around this mentality, and it molded me in my younger years. It made me disciplined, hardworking, and determined, but it also made me extreme. It made me feel special, but there was also a dark side to professional sports.

My dad was often depressed because of the media attention, and I had some pretty sad Monday mornings as a kid, when my dad's team lost miserably in a Sunday afternoon battle. The highs and lows of professional sports are something I have in my blood and that has molded me to be the intense person I am.

As a child, I was a competitive, high-level gymnast. I started young—at age three and a half. I was pretty talented and moved up quickly in the classes. Soon, I was in the competitive team programs. As I got older, my gymnastics excelled, but at age fourteen, I started to put on a lot of weight. My coach pulled me into a meeting room and told me I was too heavy to do well in the sport. He said I was a great athlete, but to do gymnastics, I was going to have to lose some weight.

I, of course, took this personally, instead of truly understanding the criticism. Back then, I think, coaches had a hard time articulating tactfully to pubescent girls how to lose weight for that sport.

I was crushed, hurt, devastated. I felt like a failure. I was going through puberty and had no idea how to stop the weight gain. No one was educating me or helping me to understand nutrition or how I could better fuel my body. It was just, "You are too heavy. We are going to weigh you in every week."

Me at age fourteen, the year my coach told me I was fat. Gymnastics at Queen City in Cincinnati, Ohio

From that point on, I felt I needed to be a certain weight in order to be good at anything. I don't remember all of the specifics, but I do remember buying diet pills and sprinkling weird things on my food to help me lose weight. I didn't eat badly, per se, but I was definitely eating too many calories and I was growing, two things as a gymnast that you "shouldn't do."

It's tricky with gymnastics, because you need to fuel yourself in order to train for four-hour workouts, but at the same time you have to be super-light to do them well. It's a challenge for girls going through puberty, as their appetites increase and their bodies change. This is what was happening to me. The way my coach responded to my weight gain impacted me for life.

To be clear, let me say this: *I am not a victim.* I think, if the coach knew now that his words hurt me so deeply, he never would have done that. But those words set me up for a few decades of trying to prove to myself and to the world that my body was good enough, strong enough, and awesome enough to be an athlete, to be "someone."

Also, I should mention that I have been on the coaching end of "heavier" gymnasts, and it is a very tender issue between coach and athlete. As an adult coach, we want the best for our gymnasts, but when the glaring problem is an athlete's fitness level, it puts us in a compromising position.

I guess what I'm saying is that it's a no-win situation for both coach and athlete, and the only way we can overcome this issue is to work together toward a healthy relationship with food and body image. My coach telling me I was heavy did not come from a place of disrespect or evil intention; it was just a coach being honest about what he saw.

It actually was a good thing all of this happened because it motivated me to excel in my life, to attain a major goal (winning my professional status in bodybuilding), and to achieve great success in the gymnastics world, both as a coach and as a trainer/nutritionist. So, things that hurt us really can make us stronger, build character, and help us become better people. People who have a story share.

That is why I am not at all bitter about what this coach said to me. As a matter of fact, I thank him for his words. I understand now that he didn't know how to verbalize what was blatantly obvious to him—that I was too heavy to do amazing gymnastics. I am very thankful for this, because it made my life's journey powerful and impactful, and because now I am able to help others with my story.

My gymnastics career didn't end so well...

In 1990, as a level-10 gymnast, I suffered two stress fractures in my back and was told to quit the sport. Today, stress fractures are a very common injury in gymnastics, and athletes are able to push through them. But in 1990, it was the end of a career for most gymnasts. Ironically, when I quit gymnastics, I immediately lost about ten pounds and completely stopped exercising. I moved on with my life and enjoyed other activities in high school. I stopped stressing about weight until it resurfaced again in my mid-twenties.

Looking back, I see now that gymnastics actually just increased my appetite, so when I quit,

I didn't have the desire to eat so much anymore. I also learned that going through puberty is one of the most difficult hardships on a teenage gymnast. It is so hard to lift your body up, to be in a leotard, and to be exceptionally light and quick while you are developing breasts and hips and becoming extremely hormonal. Gymnastics is most brutal for girls between the ages of twelve and fifteen. This is when the pressure to improve skills and increase difficulty of routine mounts. It's when college coaches begin to recruit talent, when your body starts to give out, and when you either excel or regress as an athlete. It's a trying time.

Well, I didn't rise to the occasion, due to my early retirement. However, I did manage to carry over those residual thoughts of inadequacy regarding my weight and my body for many years. Well into my thirties, in fact. Again, I want to stress that I feel no anger or distress toward my coach; I am not a victim nor do I possess a victim mentality. I think what I feel now is more sadness about having to go through all that, especially when I didn't have the tools to cope with it.

From what I remember, no one ever taught me about food. My mom was not a big chef (although she now says she only served me the food she did me because I was so picky). Most evenings, we ate canned corn, chicken breasts, and potatoes, or we'd have simple dinners like macaroni and cheese, boxed dinners, and foods made from soup recipes or hamburger-helper-type meals. We ate margarine, baked beans, white bread, and Toaster Strudels. My house was a processed food heaven!

I don't think my mom knew or understood at the time that these foods were laden with sodium, artificial colors, and flavorings. She was just doing her best to cook us quick meals on the go. I have the best parents in the world, and they did everything they could to help me succeed! Again, this was a case of limited resources and education.

And so, throughout my teenage years, I never had a coach or nutrition advisor who taught me the importance of nutrition and meal planning or the proper way to fuel my body. I think also, because of this, I later took my diet to extremes and went the other direction, becoming ultra-obsessed about every single piece of food I put into my body.

I think looking, back at this time in my life, I began to block out and repress thoughts of inadequacy that I felt about my body, which would later rear its ugly head as I got older.

MY COLLEGE YEARS & TEACHING LIFE

I WAS VERY THIN in college. I would bike plus walk every day to class. I also started hitting the gym a few days a week. I went to Michigan State, which had a sprawling campus, so I was walking twenty minutes to each of my classes both ways every day—that's about two to two and a half hours of walking each weekday. And I discovered something for the first time ever: a social life! As gymnasts, we are very restricted in our activities because we are always practicing. I was having a blast, and my years at Michigan State were the best ones of my life.

With my youthful metabolism, I was pretty much just eating like a "regular person": three meals a day plus snacks and some occasional college drinking. I was a slender size four without even trying... I didn't eat fast food and did eat very healthfully from all food groups. I was an active, happy and healthy, well-adjusted, and balanced college student.

As a matter of fact, at this time, I wasn't really struggling with my body. What I was really struggling with was my *skin*. I had terrible acne, which is a whole other story in itself, and I feel now as I write this that it also contributed to my later thoughts of not being good enough, which led to my needing to find ways to make myself better. (i.e., if I couldn't have a perfect face, I would have a perfect body!)

I remember a young boy I was babysitting said to me, "What happened to your face?" He was just a five- or six-year-old kid, but I was so ashamed, I hid behind my hair and lots of makeup after that comment. I haven't really thought about how that impacted me until I wrote this book, but now I see it also added to my body-image issues and the desire to excel in everything I did.

After I graduated from college and started to do a teaching internship, I began to put on a little weight, because I wasn't walking every day for two hours. I scheduled a doctor's appointment for a checkup in the summer of 1997.

I was twenty-three years old at that point, and my weight was 129 pounds—ten pounds heavier than I'd weighed the year before. My doctor told me I had gained ten pounds, a pattern that would continue if I didn't start working out and making lifestyle changes.

My thoughts were...

"Wait! I'm *fat* again?"

"I thought I fixed this. I'm not fat...! Well, I'll show him who's fat!"

All of a sudden, this news triggered a memory of my coach telling me I was too heavy. All of those feelings of inadequacy came rushing back to my brain from ten years before....

I immediately began a strenuous workout regime to make sure I would *NEVER* be called fat again. (Of course, my doctor did not say I was fat, but that is exactly what I *heard* him say.)

Since I had residual effects of the "you are too heavy to do gymnastics" comments on my mind, I always had it in the back of my head that I had something to prove. When I started working out again during this point, I was on a mission.

And so my body became super-lean; adding weight training only propelled me to a higher fitness level. I loved how I felt. I became extremely regimented, hitting the gym every day for two hours after work. I really was in great shape and was loving how I felt. I was back in my old gymnastics routine and feeling amazing.....

That year, I became a high school English teacher, and to stave off stress, I started running and working out even more religiously. I was getting super-fit as my old gymnastics muscles were reignited. I was super-motivated by my results and made exercising a priority in my life. People in the gym began to notice my dedication, my motivation, and my body transformation. I will admit I was feeling pretty awesome.

Finally, when someone suggested I compete in bodybuilding, my healthy lifestyle habit stopped being a habit and became an obsession. I saw the changes and began to diet harder. My body transformed very quickly. I became very lean, very muscular, and vascular; my skin was paper-thin, I thought it was so cool. I was seriously considering competing in a fitness competition or doing fitness modeling. Back then, we had no Instagram or Facebook to post selfies. If so, you would have seen many selfie photos of me posing! I was hooked.

At this point in my journey, I was ready to prove to the world that I could be someone special and take care of some "unfinished business," as my athletic career ended short and, to me, I was a failure. When we are in our twenties, we are still developing our identity and searching for who we truly are. This was a huge period of growth for me, and I'm proud of the discipline I showed.

MY TRAGIC NEAR-DEATH EXPERIENCE

IN 2001, IN THE MIDST of all of the exercising and dieting, I had a near-death experience. I suffered a transverse venous thrombosis in my brain (a blood clot), and I almost died. We never found out why I had this clot in my brain, being that I was a very healthy, in shape twenty-seven-year-old woman, but the brain is an interesting and inexplicable organ. Since I was so healthy, fit, and had no blood issues, the doctors struggled to find answers as to why this had happened to me. Birth control pills seemed to be the only potential culprit....

Afterwards, the only thing they could say was that, since I was so fit and in shape, I had been able to survive this massive blood clot. Anyone else may have died. So it was my health that kept me alive, including the strength of my heart and my will to live.

Thinking back, I can't believe I almost died. I remember my husband's family and my parents standing over my in the ICU, praying for my life. At twenty-seven, so young and with so much to live, I had to fight hard to make it out of that hospital. In my mind, I was just beginning my journey.

It is pretty scary to be twenty-seven years old and be in the ICU for days, not knowing if you will survive. I was totally confused and shell-shocked by this very terrible experience. I remember thinking, this really may be it. I may die here in this hospital and never know my life after the age of twenty-seven. I'd never know my children, never see the world, never accomplish all of my dreams, or see my family again. It was earth shattering and a huge wake-up call to how I was living my life and for whom.

I was teaching high school English at the time, and had been doing so for six years. I knew that I wasn't doing what I was supposed to be doing, as I was unfulfilled and frustrated by the politics of teaching.

When I came out of this near-death experience and when I heard what the doctors had to say, I decided I wanted to change my direction in teaching. I began to work toward getting a personal training certification. It wasn't Shakespeare that I loved. Fitness and training were my passion. Why was I teaching people about English literature when I could be teaching people about being fit? After seeing my life flash before my eyes, I knew I had to make a change in the direction of my career.

It was a long recovery. I'd lost twenty pounds off of my 130-pound frame, and I was weak, but I hit the gym hard. Amazingly, I had no residual effects. The blood clot dissolved into my brain. The clot was on my eye center and compressed down onto my optic nerve, leaving me cross-eyed and with double vision for three months. I had a hard time walking without help and needed care from my mom and husband for a couple of months.

Eventually, I was able to regain my strength and start to study to become a fitness trainer. I was so happy to be out of that high school and in a gym where I felt like I was home! I was definitely in the right place.

Since I had a teaching background, I really excelled in training. I truly cared about my clients and spent eight hours a day training people from five in the morning to nine at night. It was my passion and my goal to help people get fit like I was. I wanted to help people feel the way I did.

In addition I was able to spend all of my free time in the gym working out. I did this religiously.

Did I say religiously?

I meant to say *OBSESSIVELY.*

It was starting to get scary.

I started to spend hours and hours in the gym, doing cardio and weight training, plus teaching fitness classes. I became obsessed with calories, macros (fats, proteins, carbs) and meal planning.

This was the beginning of my obsessive years with fitness.

It was during this time that my healthy hobby turned into an unhealthy, extreme way of living that would lead me down the road to binge eating.

THE OBSESSIVE YEARS

AS A PERSONAL TRAINER, I was able to set my own schedule and move everything around my workouts and meal planning. A typical day in my dieting life would be:

* Cardio, first thing in the morning for one hour.

* Eat oatmeal and egg whites.

* Train clients and snack on almonds and raisins, yogurt, and fruit.

* Train more clients.

* Do my one-hour weight training workout.

* Train more clients.

* Eat my pre-made tuna-and-broccoli meals.

* After that, I would do another cardio session for an hour.

So that was *THREE* hours of working out, with dieting in between, PLUS training clients, all in a typical day. Not to mention, there were days when I would go home, hop on my bike, and do another hour of cardio in addition to that!

My job as a trainer allowed me to spend long days and hours in the gym. I became pretty obsessed with keeping my body lean and it started to close off my friendships. Also, my relationship with my husband became strained. We didn't have kids, so I was able to spend more and more time in the gym working on my obsession. Any extra time I had was dedicated to cardio, weights, or reading about diets, exercise strategies, or ways to compete in fitness.

All this time, I was tracking every piece of food that went into my body, every calorie, and every calorie burned. Even today, I have dozens of notebooks in my basement filled with hours of logged cardio sessions, foods eaten, calories burned, and crazy math equations of fat pounds lost and muscle gains. I read every book I could get my hands on regarding fitness, like how to add muscle and how to lose fat.

Actual pages from one of my many calorie crazy diary entries in 2004

I also worked with nutritionists who created diets for me. I was taking supplements like ephedrine, fat burners, creatine, and glutamine, protein powder, liver tabs, and amino acids. I would spend hours researching foods, diets, and supplements, looking online for calculations of exact macros and calories I needed to eat. It took over my life.

I was on a quest for the perfect body... and I wasn't quite sure why... but I found I was good at it, and people were asking me for advice on how I was doing it. I *was* doing it... but with an extreme twist, more than I should have been, and I was sacrificing time with my friends and family. But it was my job to be a trainer, so I continued.

During this time, I stopped getting my period. I also lost all desire for human or sexual contact. I also became addicted to sugar-free gum, which I didn't know at the time was destroying my stomach, making me constipated. So I also started relying on stimulant laxatives to go to the bathroom. (Not for any weight loss reason; simply to go....) This is truly embarrassing to admit, but again, I know there are many women out there who have done this exact thing. If I can help them, I will. At one point, I thought I would be addicted to laxatives my whole life. I think actually what was happening is that I had little to no waste in my body. I was burning over 6,000 calories a day.

I was eating very healthy, including lots of fruits, vegetables, and protein, but because I was so hungry from the extreme dieting and exercise, I was going through two packs of cinnamon sugarless gum a day. My digestive system was becoming a wreck! On the outside, I was looking great, but my insides were taking a beating.

I started to prepare for competitions and do photo shoots, since everyone in the gym was telling me how amazing I looked. My business started to soar: I was the most sought-after trainer in the gym. I definitely was talented at training and really did care about my clients. However, at that point, I would do anything to maintain that image of the perfect body and perfect trainer, so I continued to over-exercise, over-diet, and continue on my way. I also was spending hundreds and thousands of dollars on my upkeep, which included hair extensions, nails, tanning, facials, and waxing. It was becoming a total body project!

The beginning of the obsessive years, 2003
(Photo by Amir Mirandi)

Eventually, three hours of exercise a day began to take a toll on my head. My diet became even more restrictive, allowing just fish and green vegetables and oatmeal. The pressure to be perfect started to mount—put on by myself, of course—but I thrived on this pressure.

FITNESS COMPETITIONS

I DIDN'T REALIZE IT then, but my fitness competitor days were a direct correlation with my feelings that I had unfinished business in my gymnastics career. I wanted to prove both to myself and to my gymnastics coaches that I wasn't a fat girl who couldn't succeed. That is why I started to compete in fitness competitions—each of which included a two-minute gymnastics routine. At age twenty-nine, I was ready to prove my past wrong.

A typical fitness-competitor's diet involved lots of whitefish, green vegetables, a gallon of water, and protein shakes, with an occasional grapefruit and sweet potato here and there. That's it! Not a lot of variety.

My meal plan started to look like this; if I were ever to go off this plan, I would panic. I brought my Tupperware full of chicken, fish, and broccoli everywhere I went, even to people's houses when I was invited over for dinner. Even when I went *out* to dinner!

I would get angry or upset if an event happened to throw me off my eating schedule. I became mean with my husband at this time—the poor guy. He just wanted a wife to go out to dinner with him. But my diet was my central focus of my life and so was my body. How selfish!

In addition to my exhaustive hours of exercise, I would spend many more hours reading about bodybuilding, supplements, and different exercises. I was taking my passion to the next level and shutting out everyone in my life.

It was during this time that my first marriage started to crumble. I was married to a very amazing man then. He was supportive of my fitness, but he also wanted a family, something I wanted *NOTHING* to do with at *that* time.

Looking back, my obsessive relationship with food, exercise, and bingeing ultimately was the end of our thirteen years together. I was always putting my diet first, my training first, and *ME* first, before him. We had grown apart, and I was too selfish to compromise.

I had become so selfish that, when his father died, I stayed with my parents in a nearby hotel so I could work out on the morning of his funeral, because the hotel had a gym. Instead of staying with my husband the night before his dad's funeral, I chose to stay close to a gym...

It's pitiful. Looking back now, I am disgusted with what I did and how I was thinking. It literally makes me sick with guilt, and I have asked God for forgiveness for this terrible choice I made. How terribly selfish and egotistical I had become?

One of the most painful parts of writing this book is telling that story, but it is the truth. Again, it is an honest window into my state of my mind at that time.

When the competitions began, I moved up pretty quickly and found success early on. This only propelled me to do more dieting, with more restrictions, and more exercising. I would spend hours on Sundays preparing my meals for the week ahead: weighing my portions, cooking, and putting together perfectly aligned containers of egg whites, whitefish, asparagus, grapefruits, and oatmeal, all ready for the next seven days. Sounds healthy right?

The culture of fitness competitions is special. Do you ever wonder a little why women feel the need to get ultra-tanned, ultra-ripped, and then walk on stage in clear heels, fake hair, and sequined bikinis? Looking back, I see again that this was all part of my perfect showcase for getting back at my doubters and for showing the world I wasn't a fat girl who was no good and couldn't succeed.

Of course, my motivation was clearly distorted. I had no idea at the time, but looking back now, I see I was way too sensitive and hard on myself and insecure. I had something to prove.

The bodybuilding shows were awesome. I got to do a two-minute gymnastics routine *and* show off my tanned and perfectly toned body. Now, if that isn't a way to get back at my unfinished gymnastics career, I don't know of a better way.

I am super-proud of myself and what I did. It takes a lot of discipline to pack your food every day and workout for three hours a day religiously plus do gymnastics at age thirty-five! Although I speak not so fondly of my experience with fitness competitions, I have great respect for what I accomplished, alongside many others who are champions in the sport. (Some may not consider it a sport.)

I met a lot of friends and mentors during this time who saw my extremes coming on hard. Even to other fitness competitors, they saw me way out of balance and headed for disaster. I did listen to them but knew my journey was different than theirs, so I continued with my obsessive ways.

Pretty soon, the competitor lifestyle was too extreme for me to handle. I started to think I was missing out on all the fun and missing out on food! People seemed so happy while I felt so sad and depressed! I had to ask myself am I really doing all of this for a hobby? What do I have to prove to the world and myself? I may have the best body in the room, but do I have the best marriage? The best friendships? Or am I sitting here alone with ripped abs and no one to share them with?? It sounds funny now, but it was the sad truth.

I kept pushing through the shows, however—and began to notice that, after the shows, I wanted to do just one thing. EAT. EAT... *EAT*!!!

The restricting was starting to add up, and I was feeling anxious, sad, and unhappy. But what could I do? I was getting closer and closer to my professional status in the IFBB, and so I had to push on...

THE BEGINNING OF THE BINGES

I REMEMBER THE FIRST time I went on a real eating binge.

I had heard about it but was pretty sure it would never happen to me. Until it did. It was a terrible binge. I ate a loaf of bread and a jar of peanut butter, followed by five or six bags of popcorn. This was after a dinner out with friends.

My stomach was so distended, my body swollen with water, I wanted to throw up, but I had no gag reflex when I stuck my finger down my throat. (I realize now I would have been a bulimic, but I don't have a gag reflex.)

Trust me when I say that I *cannot* make myself throw up. I tried many, many, many times. I remember someone telling me once that they had to buy Ipecac for their dog, to make him throw up after he ingested poison. So I went to the store and bought some. It didn't work. I was miserable. And I was ashamed that I had gone to such a drastic measure.

Imagine doing restrictive dieting for four to five months at a time. Imagine the effect it has on the body, the mind, the brain. Can you imagine what happens after putting a little salt in that body, a little processed food, or *A LOT* of these things?

My body had lost the sensation and hormonal effects of sugar, salt, fat. So when I put *one* bite of sugar, salt, or fat into myself, I would blow up like a balloon.

After my shows, I would binge for days and gain between ten and fifteen pounds of water in a week. This took me years to correct. For about four years after I quit bodybuilding, I would continue to struggle with water retention and a slow metabolism. The constant dieting had destroyed my metabolism. My calorie counts each day were so low before competitions that, when I would go on three- or four-day benders afterwards, my body would shut down. It would hold all of the fat, salt, and water, to the point that I had to take water pills, dandelion root, and laxatives.

Every time I did this, I would gain twenty to thirty pounds. I would lose it quickly, but each time it got harder and harder to do so. I was slowly killing my metabolism with all of these extreme weight changes.

2006—the binging begins. Nightly visits to the breadbasket!

This type of bingeing and dieting went on from 2004 until 2010. Throughout this time period, I lost thirty pounds and gained thirty pounds no less than six times. That is like going through six pregnancies in six years and doing bodybuilding competitions in between each pregnancy. That is how extreme my situation truly was.

It was a nightmare. I was out of balance, out of control; a slave to food, diet, and exercise. Unable to enjoy food like other people. I was locked in a cycle of binge and restriction. And I couldn't get out.

CHICAGO: THE BEST AND WORST OF TIMES—MY BINGING SECRETS

IN 2004, MY HUSBAND got a great job in Chicago, and so we moved there. I was excited, ready to move somewhere new, but also deeply into my fitness competitions at the time.

We packed up everything and moved from Columbus, Ohio to Chicago, where I got a job in a fancy fitness club downtown. The gym was located in the Aon Center, which is a building right in the heart of the city filled with very important businesses and tons of fast food restaurants that people would frequent for morning coffee and lunch.

I remember being in Chicago, training clients, and then walking through the Aon Center, where I would constantly smell the bagels and bread and breakfast sandwiches. All I could think about all morning while training clients was what I would eat. Then I would go home and gorge myself ...

During this time, I would go on weekly food marathons, where I would call in sick and work from my computer. I hid myself away behind my computer screen while I binged on peanut butter, honey, butter, and oat mixtures, because these were the permissible, "clean" foods in my house. I still refused to buy junk. Remember, I was still competing at this time and doing the "thirty pounds up and thirty pounds down" dance.

In Chicago, I would often create crazy combinations of foods. My husband was always working, so I spent a lot of time alone. I had tons of clean food in my house, so I thought I could eat clean and be okay... but I was making all sorts of crazy concoctions with them, to satisfy my bingeing needs.

I also started hitting up fast-food drive-throughs and restaurants in secret. Multiple ones in one- to two-hour windows of time.

One day, after a bodybuilding show, I drove through a McDonald's and ordered a McGriddle sandwich—pancakes with syrup and sausage loaded in the middle. Then I went to another drive-in and had another, and then I drove to another. I figured I would then go through another fast-food drive-thru, so I continued. That is four drive-throughs, and I am not exaggerating. That is how a binge eater operates.

It was a drug... Food was becoming an addiction. Food was more of a physiological need than a mental need. It wasn't the desire to taste food: I didn't enjoy it; I just wanted that "high" from the sugar buzz, the control, and from thinking I could eat whatever I wanted and no one could stop me!

I would eat myself to sleep then have to take a warm bath to relax me, because I was literally sore, my stomach distended, my body hot and sweaty as I made my metabolism and organs work in overdrive. When you binge, some crazy person steps into your soul and takes over your body. You are in a trance. And although your head is saying, "*STOP!* This is *crazy,*" your hand continues to reach for more food to shove in your mouth. You feel possessed.... It's unreal.

Why was I doing this? Was I hungry? Naturally, the deprivation of carbs and fat over long periods of time led me to have an insatiable appetite for both sugar and salt. I was also craving fat, because I had deprived myself for so long. I had a fascination with butter. I mean *sticks* of raw butter, which I would slather on bread or melt and add oats to. I would eat whole sushi boats that had been made to feed four people. I would go on weekly house lock-ins, where I would eat, eat, and eat, sleep and do no exercise.

My work as a personal trainer suffered, and I became depressed. I couldn't face my clients, who would see me go from a 125-pound shredded bodybuilder to a soft, 155-pound woman with a swollen face.

You may not believe a typical day of post-show bingeing, but it looked like this:

First, wake up with a new attitude. I'd begin by eating a Balance protein bar. (I thought this would be a healthy start, but protein bars are loaded with sugar and this made me want *more*.)

Then I would have two, three, four more Balance bars, and finally eat five to six of them. (Again, this is embarrassing to write, as these are my deepest, darkest bingeing secrets.) However, I really want my readers to understand the extent to which a binge eater goes to get food into their body.

After the protein bars, I would stop by a grocery store buffet or salad bar, where I would load up on pasta salads, olives, cheeses, crackers, breads, cookies. I took a little bit of everything. You know those people who load up on the buffet so there is no more room on the plate? Mine looked like Mt. Rainier!

After I was so stuffed, I would follow this with a nap. When I awoke, I would be sweating... and right then, I would start ordering sushi rolls and go walk to pick them up (we lived in downtown).

Then, as I walked around downtown Chicago, I would search for desserts like pies, muffins, and processed baked goods like cheese danishes, Cinnabons, bagels, and cookies. Or sometimes I would order pizza and breadsticks and eat them all until I was so sick I couldn't move.

Again, I am not in any way exaggerating my daily activities. In fact, I remember thinking to myself, *WHAT THE HELL?? I am crazy*!!

I also remember thinking, one day, I would write about this.

If you have ever binged, you know what it feels like to be in a trance. It's like an out-of-body experience that takes ahold of you. I always knew that gluttony was one of the seven deadly sins, but I never imagined that, for seven years, I would go through a binge-eating disorder.

I would eat all of the food in the house that my husband bought and then go to the store and quickly replace it all, so he wouldn't know what I'd done. I would wake up in middle of the night and "sleep eat." I would go to the cupboard, pull out loaves of bread, slather the slices with peanut butter and jelly, then melt cheese on bagels, and eat until I was sick. I would eat bowls and bowls of cereal and oatmeal, adding brown sugar, butter and peanut butter—any combinations I could make or find in the kitchen. Bags of chips, pretzels, and then popcorn. Can you say *popcorn*?? Bags and bags and bags with my real melted butter drenched all over the kernels.

If you think this is bad, things got even worse while I was going through my divorce in 2007.

Before the divorce, I tried to save the marriage by making my husband happy. He desperately wanted children, and I was resisting. Plus, I hadn't had a period in about five years. So I decided to temporarily quit dieting and competing and try to have a child. I did about eight months of fertility injections, pills, artificial insemination, and frequent fertility treatments to try to get pregnant. I wasn't doing it for me; I was doing it for him. We failed numerous times in the venture, and I gained even more weight during this time due to the hormone injections and other pills. I became resentful and binged even more during this time out of depression, resentment, and unhappiness.

There were moments when I ate so much, I couldn't breathe, and then I ate more. Yes, I felt so sick, but I also felt so empty. I wanted to keep filling the hole inside of me with carbs and fat and junk. I couldn't stop.

The only thing that got me to stop my binges was complete and total exhaustion. It was like doing a four-hour workout, but instead it was a twelve-hour sport of "eating." My stomach hurt, my skin hurt, my ribs hurt, and my ab muscles hurt from being distended. I was constipated, bloated, water retained, swollen, *MISERABLE*. I could barely walk.

I hid myself away during these darkest moments, shut off my phone and social media, and hibernated in my lonely one-bedroom apartment in downtown Chicago. It was the scene of a disaster movie, only I was the person, me alone, who was destroying myself.

I remember playing weird games and making strange combinations with foods. For instance, I thought it was okay to eat oatmeal, as it was healthy. I would start with putting some butter in a pan, then I would put some dry oats on the stove. I would toast the oats until they were crunchy and brown. Then I would scoop them in my mouth.

Then I would get bored with that and add more butter. Then some honey. Then some cinnamon. Then some nuts. Pretty soon, I had created my own granola. Then I would add some cocoa powder. Then add some whipped cream. (Right now, I am laughing at this, but it's all true! I was getting really creative with this stuff.)

This may sound weird, but many binge eaters do this: they create food mixtures with the food they have around their homes, tricking themselves into believing they are bingeing on "healthy foods." I was so ashamed. Thinking back on this now makes me cringe. But I was hurting so bad...

In making these creations, I started with a healthy food with the intention of adding just a little butter and then it would snowball out of control. This is the perfect metaphor for my daily relationship with food. I had the best intentions every day, but then it escalated out of control. Once that sugar hit my system and my blood sugar elevated, the desire for more sugar began yet again.

I would start with a chocolate bar. And then a peanut butter cup. And then two more bars and two more peanut butter cups. And then, when I ran out of food options, I would go to the local Walgreens and buy more processed snacks, like cheese danish, chocolate-covered pretzels, chocolate-covered raisins, and Pringle sticks, Cheetos, plus loaves of bread with butter and cinnamon and sugar.

I would literally eat myself into a food coma. I was so out of control, I often did not recognize my bloated, swollen face and puffy eyes the next day.

I would continue this type of bingeing for weeks and months, and it was extremely painful to come out of these benders—my addiction was so strong that I didn't care. I was afraid I was never going to be able to eat bad food again, because I knew a very strict diet would be coming, so I gorged myself on the forbidden.

When you are told you can't eat something or shouldn't eat something, it triggers the response of "*I want more of that*, because it is forbidden!"

The forbidden and the permitted food cycle created a monster. I didn't know who I was anymore. I thought about food all day long and what I would binge on next.

I would look up restaurants and recipes online while I should have been working. I perused grocery store aisles, looking for foods that would satisfy my deepest bingeing need. How much more food and how many more combinations could I take down?

Even though I was embarrassed with my appearance, I didn't care, because I had my fitness pictures to prove I really was fit. This wasn't in fact me! I was really a *skinny* person inside, and I knew I could lose the weight quickly through lots of exercise and extreme dieting. I had done it five or six times before. Little did I know that I was wreaking havoc on my metabolic system, something that would take years to fix.

The worst part about this cycle in my life was the guilt and depression. Not only was the physical aspect of it a strain, but so was the mental. I would binge and then hide it, feel guilty, and have to hide from the world. I would binge for a few days then have days of four to six hours of secretive exercise, where I would call in sick to work or not show up to my clients' sessions because I was so waterlogged. I would sit in the sauna, get full-body wraps to pull out the water, and take water pills and laxatives. I would go on cleanses and detoxes. I remember one day I did six hours of cardio, *IN A ROW*.

My view of fitness became deeply distorted. I was obsessed with food on one hand and dieting severely on the other.

Can you imagine being a personal trainer as well as a binge-eating cardio bulimic? I was dying of guilt behind the facade I had to put on. Soon, I couldn't even face my clients....

One of my more interesting rituals would be to go out to dinner with friends and order something extremely healthy, to appear to be a "fit person"—after all, I *was* a personal trainer. But when I would get home, I would eat for hours, especially after my husband went to bed.

I found myself replacing food early in the morning more and more frequently, so my husband wouldn't see (for instance) that I'd eaten an entire loaf of bread or stick of butter. The sleep-eating became a problem, too. Sometimes, I would find myself in the kitchen at three or four in the morning, eating... Possessed.... I had no idea what I was doing. I realized I had a problem, but I couldn't or didn't want to stop.

You may wonder at this point how did this happen. I wasn't abused; I had a great childhood, supportive parents, was never neglected, and had every opportunity for education and training that I'd ever wanted. I had great friends and family and self-esteem. I had money, a good life, and a nice husband.

So, how did such a normal, well-balanced, and well-adjusted person become a food addict and binge eater? I had to dig really deep to find the answers, and when I did, it was very surprising.

WINNING MY PRO CARD AND DIVORCE

ONE OF THE PROUDEST moments of my life came when I won my pro card in fitness in Chicago in 2008. I was so proud of myself because I had achieved the ultimate level in body fitness: winning my Professional Status in the IFBB.

I'm a Pro NOW! 2008 Pro Card Win, Chicago

If you don't know what the IFBB is, it is the International Federation of Bodybuilding and Fitness. It is the most highly acclaimed and sought-after professional status, if you are competing in the bodybuilding world.

It took me about three and a half years to get my pro card, which is not very long, because I accelerated rather quickly. I was determined, focused, and obsessed on this goal. The problem was that doing so took away from my personal life, my marriage, and my relationships.

The three to four hours a day of working out and living on a detailed meal-planning schedule took me away from social outings, vacations, and enjoying life. My husband at the time wanted to start a family, go out to dinners, take nice vacations, and enjoy our life together.

But I wasn't having it. I was so focused on winning that pro card that I would not attend his work dinners, and I would skip outings and stay at home while he was out with our friends. I was very isolated by my choices and extremely out of balance. At the time, I didn't see it or understand it. Looking back now, it's not as if I was wrong; it was just where my heart was at the time,

This caused huge stress in my marriage. All I wanted was for my husband to understand where I was at that point in my life, which was focused on a fitness dream. I can take most of the responsibility now, as I pushed him away, but I also feel that he should have let me pursue my dreams in fitness, because I had a burning desire, and, well, that was my path and my journey.

Because of my extreme yo-yo lifestyle, I was depressed and unstable and unhappy. Everyone knew it.

Finally, my husband had had enough. I was all over the place: one minute, bingeing; the next minute, exercising and eating clean. It was like living with a bi-polar person who was not on medication and was living in denial.

Sadly, we split up. My fitness "life" was the reason why. He has since gone on to a happy marriage with a nice family and is very content. I have gone on, as well. Now, I'm a wife and mother, so all is good, in the end. But I see how this divorce made me truly comprehend how my obsessions were affecting my relationships and contributing to my inability to connect.

We split up in the fall of 2007, and in 2008, I won my pro card in fitness. We were heavy into our divorce at that point. I remember sitting in our lawyer meetings, going over paperwork, and telling my soon-to-be-ex that I had just gotten my pro card in fitness. He was legitimately happy for me, but I knew our divorce was the direct result of my win.

After the divorce and winning my pro card, I dove head-deep into three years of hardcore food bingeing, depression, self-loathing, partying, and sadness.

I had lost all desire to compete at that point, and my husband was gone. I was alone, sad, bingeing, and out of control. This was the lowest point of my life.

GETTING FAT

(*Recovery Mode, But I Didn't Know It*)

THE FIRST STEPS in my recovery took about two years. I actually didn't know I was in the recovery stage of my disorder at that time.

First, I stopped dieting and stopped restricting. I decided to quit competing, because it wasn't what I wanted to do with my life. I was over it!

I allowed myself to eat everything I wanted, and I gained a ton of weight. I think I got up to 180 pounds.

2009—my brother's wedding, one year after my pro card win. Bingeing out of control!

If I wanted a beef and cheddar, I ate it. If I wanted a cheese danish, I ate it. I did all this knowing that there would be no excessive exercising or restrictive dieting for weeks afterward, to get me back to normal weight.

I realized that, this time, I was going to exercise normally afterward and just see what happened. (Mind you, normally was two hours a day!) I never stopped working out during this point, and so I stayed super-strong. I think my consistency with training during this time helped me maintain some sort of shape and fitness. I was still strong and happy to work out.

I maintained this routine for about three years. I would both eat and drink a lot of alcohol with my meals. At this point, I had moved back to Cincinnati (my hometown) and started to coach gymnastics at Cincinnati Gymnastics, an amazing gymnastics center that would build the foundation of my success later in my career. I wanted out of the bodybuilding world and was looking for something fresh and new, where I could use my fitness expertise in a job that was separate from straight fitness.

I was lucky enough to hook on with Mary Lee Tracy, an Olympic gymnastics coach and an extremely respectable one at that. Mary Lee allowed me to come into CGA and develop my conditioning ideas into more gymnastics-based movements. She also allowed me to develop a clean-eating program within her gym, which was the beginning of my developing the programs I use today with athletes.

I found some friends and started to become more social. As I became more social and went out more, I started to actually eat foods that I would have never eaten before, like steak, crab legs, pasta, bread, and chocolate desserts. There was no limit—I was game to try it all.

You see, my relationship with food was changing yet again. Food started to become my coping strategy for stress, for poor relationships, my divorce. It became almost a hobby. The thing that had was once been "forbidden" became the be all and end all of my fantasies. I chose food before personal interactions. I chose food before shopping, I chose food before getting my hair done, relaxing, or traveling. All I could think about was what would I have at the end of the day? I would starve myself all day in anticipation of the nightly feast. It was a reward for all the pain in my life.

When I went into the "let myself get fat mode," I was partying a lot with another woman who was also battling some relationship woes and depression. We would get drinks after work three or four times a week, downing Long Island Iced Teas, and eat at Outback Steakhouse three times a week. It was our stress reliever.

And I didn't care. I was still working out every day, but I pretty much allowed myself to eat whatever I wanted. I was eating without thinking, including baked potatoes with butter and lots of bread and desserts. It wasn't all bad. I did have some fun times, but the pounds were packing on. I was probably around 165-170 pounds at this point—about twenty-five pounds over a healthy weight for me.

When I was finished eating out at a restaurant, I would continue... Chocolate, nuts, peanut butter, bread. The gorge fest continued until late into the evening.

The next morning would be hell. I was swollen, puffy, bloated, and depressed. And so I would jump on the treadmill for an hour or two, trying to push out all of that water out of my swollen face, swollen ankles, and bloated belly. I was constipated, fluffy, fat (for me), and miserable.

But the cycle continued, because, as I was exercising, I was constantly thinking about what I would eat later that night. Pretty crazy, huh? The whole reason *WHY* I started binging in the first place had been forgotten.

I initially started binging because I felt restricted by food and so I wanted to rebel. But now I was bingeing because it was a reward and I didn't know how to find my old self.

I was a slave to food. It controlled my every thought and move, and I didn't even know or understand why. I was on a food high for a long time; for years, I never thought I would come out of it. I thought I would be a binge eater forever, and I started to accept that I would never be fit again. And this devastated me... I knew this wasn't really who I was, but at the same time I just accepted and gave in to it. I decided it was my lifestyle to be this way and kept right on living with it. I stopped putting pressure on myself to change.

I was not happy in my own skin, however, as a regular woman. I didn't even want to be a bodybuilder anymore or perfect. I just wanted to look decent in a bathing suit or a pair of jeans. I lived in baggy sweatshirts, yoga pants, and T-shirts. I stopped wearing makeup or caring really about how I looked. I was officially unhappy with my body. I was supposed to be a trainer and yet I didn't look like one or eat like one or want to be one.

I did want to change, but I was addicted to food, and, ironically, counseling people on how to eat at the same time. Just because I had a degree, some pictures, and was a "PRO" bodybuilder, I seemingly had the right to counsel others on how to "eat," but I was failing myself. I felt like a failure, ashamed; the guilt was killing me.

At one point, I was so desperate to find the answer to my problem that I read every self-help book on the market with the topic of binge eating.

Jeanine Roth was very instrumental in explaining things for me through her books. I listened to every single one of them. They didn't help me at the time, but they would later.

I didn't realize it at then, because I wasn't really ready to change, but years later I would come to understand that what she was saying to be true. Once I let go of trying to control food and listened to my intuitive needs, what my body was craving, I did actually change. But I changed *back* to the person I always was. It was a "finding my old self" journey that cured me.

At my core, I was a healthy person. I just let the obsessive world of perfection control my every desire. For a long time, I was trying too hard to be perfect, and when I couldn't get there, I just threw in the towel and gave up. In my mind, if you can't be perfect, then why even try to be "good"? If you can't hit the top, then anything less is a failure.

That is the mindset that I had to overcome.

There is a Will Ferrell Movie called *Talladega Nights*. In it, the character Ricky Bobby always lived by his dad's words: "If you ain't first, you're last." I was living that is the type of mentality, too: all or nothing. If I wasn't going to be perfect, then I might as well just suck!

Later in the movie, Ricky's dad tells him that this type of thinking is stupid! In fact, he was high when he gave him that stupid advice!!

It doesn't matter if you are first, second, third, or last. It's your heart, intentions, and integrity that count the most. I had to find this out the hard way, but eventually I would.

During this time, I was dating a younger man, someone who supported me but who didn't want to commit to me long term. This made me uneasy, unhappy, and insecure. It compounded my obsessive bingeing and made me depressed and unsatisfied. He was a super-nice guy and was there for me during a tough time, but the relationship was also strained. I was having a hard time loving myself, so the foundation of it was weak. There were trust issues and lots of miscommunication; it just wasn't the right fit at the right time. I was not able to handle a serious relationship yet.

THE AUTHORS WHO SAVED ME

AT ABOUT THIS TIME, I started to see a psychologist to get the root of my eating disorder. I wanted to know why I was so depressed, sad, wanting food all the time, and unsuccessful in my relationships. Why had food become my drug??

Jeanine Roth, Pema Chödrön, and Deepak Chopra: these writers were all instrumental in my deep search within. It was deep and dark, but I bought their books on CD and listened to them over and over on my fifty-minute car commute to work every day. I cried every single day. It was true therapy.

These authors helped me achieve balance, live in the moment, and search into the *why* of my bingeing. I listened to their words of advice, and searched within to find out why I was living. Why was I here? What good did I have to give to this world, other than my body and my fitness knowledge? Surely there had to be more.

During this time, I also met with sport psychologist Dr. Alison Arnold, who also worked with gymnasts. I was able to connect with her and share my issues, and we developed a connection. She truly helped me "live in the moment" and reach for my "best me." She influenced me in many ways during this time, and we had many one-on-one sessions that helped me push through my addiction. She told me I had to *"Go Through* the pain, to get *Through* the pain..."

Eventually, I started to really *hate* food, and I became angry about its power over me. I didn't even want to even eat anymore. I wanted to just stop eating completely.... Food addiction is tricky, though, because you actually have to eat to live.

However, with lots of focus on these books and lots of time listening to these authors, I started to see the light. Of course, I didn't stop bingeing overnight. In total, it took me about three to four years of very, very hard work to completely quit. Throughout, I was concerned it was an obstacle I might never be able to overcome.

I remember asking myself, "Will I always have this problem? When will I be normal like everyone else, like people who can eat their food and then stop and go on with their life? When will I stop obsessively thinking about bread, butter, and carbs?"

I remember watching people who weren't *fit* but skinny, eating carbs and fat in moderation, and thinking, *Why can't that be me?*

Why can't I just eat a baked potato or a plate of pasta and stop?

Why can't I STOP??

I know what to do!! Why can't I do it???

What I didn't realize at the time, but realize now, is that I was physiologically addicted to food; it was now both mental and physical. Why was I seeking out the loving embrace of food?

I dug deep and found my answers:

* I was chasing perfection from my gymnastics days and repressed body image issues

* I was sad about my failed marriage

* I was living alone.

* I was ashamed and guilt-ridden.

* I was lost.

All of these things, compounded by a physiological need to eat sugar, a restrictive-diet mentality, and a long history of body shaming, made me a binge eater. But there was hope and change just around the corner...

FALLING IN LOVE WITH HEALTHY FOOD

I STOPPED EATING fast food when I was seventeen years old. Not because I was told to, but because I felt really disgusting when I ate it. While my friends were going through the drive-thru, I decided to quit.

It got even better in college. I refused any fast food or fried food. This was really where my healthy eating began. When I was at Michigan State University, I had a joke with all of my friends. There was a Taco Bell on Grand River Avenue that was always packed on every weekend night, after college students had finished their beer guzzling evenings. The Taco Bell was open twenty-four hours, and still it was always jammed!

As a freshman, I promised my friends I would never step inside the Taco Bell... and I never did— LOL! I plan to go back and visit the campus sometime soon and I still definitely will *not* be stopping in!

I loved living fast-food free. I noticed my skin was better, I felt better, and I was able to maintain my weight effortlessly, when I didn't eat fast food. Amazingly, I didn't eat fast food for ten years... And that is when I became a personal trainer. I was in love with healthy food, fruits, vegetables, lean meats, and non-processed food.

After years of compulsive eating, I wanted to get back to that person, because I knew, deep inside, that person wanted to come back. But I was so addicted to sugar and salt physiologically that I didn't know how to find my way back to the fit girl who always refused to eat fast food. I wanted to become that healthy person I truly was! I wanted to find that girl, whose true passions were fitness and clean eating. But this time, I wanted to be her on *my* terms with no restrictions.

SO, first, I got fat, as I explained earlier. Then I went through the cycle of eating whatever I wanted. During that time, I began to read a lot of self-help books and started to work on myself. In addition I stopped limiting "forbidden" foods and started to eat healthy foods that I'd restricted before (like certain fruits, vegetables, and healthy fats). You see, obsessive dieting can *CAUSE* binge eating disorder, so I had to reverse this process. I knew it was going to take time, but I hung in there and continued my quest to fall back in *love* with healthy eating.

Let me say something about food restriction and going on a diet.

The problem with food restriction and dieting is that if forces you to put foods into two categories: foods that are *Good* and foods that are *Bad*. I was putting foods like bananas, avocados, nuts, fruits, rice, potatoes, whole grain breads, and yogurt into the *Bad* category, which is absolutely untrue and crazy. But I was so brainwashed by the bodybuilding diet that I thought these healthy foods were *bad* for me!

I slowly started to integrate these foods back into my diet. Sometimes I indulged too much in the beginning, but I started to see that when I ate these foods in moderation, I began to lose weight, look better, and feel healthier. I actually started to feel like my old self again, pre-depression, pre-binge, and pre-competition.

I also started to eat a more plant-based diet, including tons of fruits and vegetables, nuts, and healthy fats... Again, things I'd restricted before, because I thought they were bad. I was now eating these foods with the freedom to do so. No one was telling me I couldn't, and I actually started to listen to my own hunger. Was I still hungry? Did I really want to eat more? Did I really want to be a fat person? Or did I want to find that healthy person who was really inside of me.

At this time, I also contacted a homeopathic doctor about my digestive issues. As I described earlier, the bingeing cycles, along with my addiction to sugar free gum, had ruined my digestive system. I was bloated, constipated, and dependent on laxatives; everything I ate stuck in my stomach. I didn't want to be taking stimulant laxatives my whole life. I was truly determined to reverse the effects of this on my system.

This doctor put me on a strict regime of bentonite clay, digestive enzymes, probiotics, colloidal silver, fish oil, and some other supplements. I truly didn't believe that these supplements could help me, but after six months, my life started to change. At first, I didn't believe I would be able to eat food and not feel bloated. I didn't believe I would be able to go to the bathroom without help... But it started to change, and I am so thankful it did....

At this point, I was nearing the end of my bingeing. I was still doing it occasionally but nowhere near the level I'd been doing it, before. The bingeing happened in episodes fewer and farther between. Over time, I became just more and more disgusted at the idea of it.

I was finding me again.

I was finding balance.

I was realizing my bingeing wasn't about food.

I wasn't dieting. I allowed myself to eat chocolate and popcorn, for example, but I stopped at a single serving. I listened to my body and began to eat *intuitively*. What did I really want to eat?

I want this or that..., and then I stopped when I was full.

It was weird because my brain was saying, "Come on. You want more! You know you want to indulge. Keep eating..."

But my body was full and, for the first time, I was listening to my body and not my distorted thoughts.

Also, around this time, I found love, which was a truly motivating factor. Did I really want to be a binge-eating, out-of-control girlfriend, wife, or mother? My perspectives on life started to change as I seriously thought about being with another man again. Did I want to be the overweight, binge-eating wife? Or did I want to be the beautiful, healthy, IFBB Pro athlete?

MOVING TO FRANCE & MARRYING A FRENCHIE

WHEN I MET MY current husband, I was at the end of my bingeing "career." Meeting him catapulted me to completely overcome the disorder. My current husband is French, and he introduced me to a whole new way of eating.

After going through a divorce in 2008, I really wanted to find a man with whom I felt comfortable and happy with in my own skin. And when I met him, I decided I wanted to be the fit woman I knew I could be.

Not just for him, but for the health of our relationship. One of the greatest things that this man brought into my life (other than my two children and a stepdaughter) was the experience of moving to and living in France. When I moved to France, my whole relationship with food changed.

Finding Balance in France

You see, the French eat everything. They eat bread, they eat cheese, they drink wine, they eat chocolate... Nothing is off-limits. Yet, they aren't overweight, and they balance their meals so beautifully. They appreciate their food, they love to cook, and they use amazing products.

I lived in the south of France, where the Mediterranean diet is king, including olives, fresh fruit, vegetables, fish, tomatoes, wine, and olive oil. Some of these foods were on my "forbidden list" before. But here, I began to find balance again, and I also started to lose weight!!

The French eat a light breakfast and a big lunch, then a small portion for dinner with a snack at 4 p.m. This type of eating was completely foreign to me, as I would skip breakfast and lunch and then gorge myself at dinner (like most Americans currently do). The French do everything in moderation and enjoy a goûter (snack) at four in the afternoon, which is coffee or tea and a sugary treat like a croissant, chocolate, eclair, etc.

The difference between the French and the American diet is this: calories. The majority of the French are not fat people. I know this because I lived there for two years and I rarely saw a fat person. Yes, they exist. But here in the States, we may see seven out of ten people who are overweight. In France, it's maybe two out of ten.

The French are balanced eaters. They eat sugar every day. They eat fat. They eat bread. How is it that we Americans are getting this so wrong? Because we are out of balance, we eat too much, work too much, stress too much, and live hard in the extreme.

Another problem here in America is that we have access to food 24/7. In France, restaurants close at 8 p.m. So do grocery stores. There are no 24-hour convenience stores or restaurants. Fast food is limited. The majority of calories are eaten earlier in the day, so they are burned off early. (While we Americans take in the bulk of our calories after 4 p.m., the French are three-quarters of the way through eating their daily calories.) Americans tend to go to bed on very full stomachs.

The French aren't stressed out about work like we are. Most of them take public transportation or ride a bike or walk to work. They get off work at 5 p.m. and have a two-hour lunch break. They don't work on Wednesdays and have a different government system (not capitalism), where the people are given the necessities to live even if they have no money. They walk everywhere. There is more stress about the weather in France, because the majority of them spend time outdoors, biking and walking, and because many jobs are government-based.

It's not better or worse, just different than our culture in America. Capitalism puts a certain amount of stress on people and causes them to indulge in food and drink.

I found that, in France, stress was centered more around relationships, competition over clothing, and worrying about what everyone else had or didn't have (jealousy), rather than on success in the workplace. Socialism affects people differently than capitalism; I didn't believe or understand that until I actually lived in it.

People in America indulge in food as a stress reliever, whereas in France more people smoke, drink, and shop (this was just my experience) to deal with stress.

In any case, I continued to exercise with these new eating principles: bread for breakfast, a large lunch, a fun snack at 4, and a small dinner.

Amazingly, in the first two months in France, I lost nine pounds. I was continuing my workouts plus walking everywhere, and I also began eating like a Frenchwoman. Wow! I couldn't believe I was drinking wine, eating cheese and chocolate, and I still lost nine pounds.

This was absolutely mind-blowing. Of course, I was eating all these things in moderation, but the French completely changed my whole perspective on food.

I also became pregnant in the fall of 2013. For years, I tried to get pregnant with my first husband but wasn't able to do so. I attribute both of my pregnancies (I gave birth again in 2016) to a balance in my hormones and a return to healthy living, eating, and being in balance and in touch with my body—from my digestive system to my mental health, the ability to not restrict, and to live a well-rounded life. These all contributed to my fertility, I am convinced.

Pregnant with No. 2, Ayden

Although I moved back to America in late 2014, due to my desire to work here and be closer to my family, I feel that living in France was hugely instrumental in helping me end my binge eating. I was able to take a good look at American culture and see how we are obsessed with food, indulgence, and extremes. It was pivotal, crucial, and instrumental in my overcoming binge eating.

MY SON LENNY...

IN MY PROCESS OF overcoming binge eating, I was also highly motivated by the fact that I became the mother of two beautiful boys, Lenny and Ayden (aka Tomato). Lenny, who was born in France, has autism. It is a very challenging to be the mother of a child with autism. I had to really look at my future and see what my son would need. First and foremost, I saw that he would need *ME*.

Lenny may need me forever. He doesn't speak, he has limited communication, and was born premature at 2.5 pounds. He is severely underweight and delayed in all areas, from fine motor skills to language, expression, and body functions.

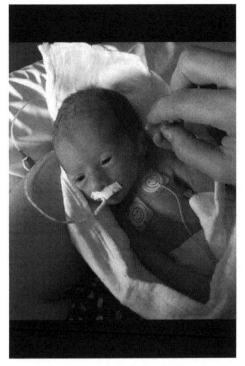

Lenny James, 2.5-pound miracle

His story is part of my story in that I never wanted children. I was so focused on and obsessed with my body and my fitness, I thought having a baby would never work for my time schedule. I didn't feel that motherly instinct to take care of children.

His story forever changed my view on who I wanted to be. Lenny was born in France on May 19, 2014. I was on bed rest the whole pregnancy, because he was measuring abnormally small. I was thirty-nine years old, living in France with no family nearby, and they told me there was something wrong with the fetus growing inside of me. I couldn't help but think that I had done something wrong to my body all of those years of extremes.

I remember bleeding the first five months of the pregnancy, going for daily ultrasounds, and praying that this little life would be okay. I cried, I prayed, and was legitimately terrified of what might happen to the life inside of me. Why was he so small? Why was I bleeding? Does he have a birth defect? Will he live?

The thought of food didn't even cross my mind other than what the doctors told me to eat, and to lie on my left side. While I was on bed rest, a nurse came to visit me two times every day, to check the baby's vitals.

Perspective. I was about to get it! Winnie the Pooh once said, "Sometimes the smallest things take up the most room in our hearts." Le petit Lenny (as the French nurses called him) was about to bring me a whole new perspective on life.

At thirty-two weeks and four days, Lenny James came into the world. He screamed so loud, the nurse said to my husband, "Was that the two-pound baby who screamed?"

That morning, I went in for an emergency C-section. Lenny's birth weight was two and a half pounds, *half* the size of a preemie born at the same age. He was even smaller than a preemie, but he was breathing and survived the umbilical cord being wrapped around his neck after a very traumatic pregnancy.

We stayed in a French hospital for the next two months, attached to machines, tube feeding the baby, and praying every night for Lenny to be a fighter.

I believe in a higher power, and that higher power gave me the best gift when He gave me

Lenny! To change from a person who selfishly put herself first for so long into a determined mother who would do anything to help her child live was a remarkable journey. My thoughts of myself totally became clear. Life had perspective. It wasn't all about me or my body. I had just given life to this amazing being. Since that time, I have completely changed my views on motherhood and food.

Lenny was not only small but he had eating issues and could not eat solid food for his first three years of life. Ironic, being my kid!! We battled during his first three years of life to get him to eat. He also had a developmental problem that we couldn't deny. He was diagnosed with autism in November of 2016, at the age of two and a half.

Ultimately, I want to be around for him. Who is going to be there for him, when he can't drive or do his bills? Who is going to help him into adulthood? Who is going to help him understand the world around him? Potty train him, help him to read, write, and function as a person in our society???

Me!!

And he can't have an unhealthy, overweight, disease-ridden, selfish lady for a mom! He needs me, and I will be there for him and do everything I can to be there for him. Binge eating, SMINGE eating!! Does that really matter anymore? *NO*!!!

Perhaps you, too, have people in your life who need you. You may not have an autistic child, but you may have children siblings, parents, or a spouse who needs you! Our families *need* us to be strong, fit, and healthy. Binge eating, like other addictions, destroys our health, our confidence, and our ability to be balanced, sound-minded people.

We need to be healthy for others if not ourselves! I hope this chapter speaks to you in ways that the others may not, because it's not about me. It's about my son. And each one of us has a family member or ten who needs us.

As someone one said, "Motherhood has the greatest potential to influence human life." Let us be examples to our children by healing or internal battles and showing great strength in our lowest times.

BETSY MCNALLY

FOOD AS A REWARD

ONE OF THE BIGGEST things that helped me overcome binge eating was looking at food as fuel and not as a reward. We eat to live; we don't live to eat. And until we can look at food as nourishment and fuel and not as a reward, we will always struggle with this.

I myself struggled because of obsessive dieting, but I know there are regular men and women who use food and alcohol to reward and relieve stress related to work or to life in general. So, even though we all have different stories, circumstances, and challenges, we are all connected by the same obsession, the same addiction to food.

The only way we can truly overcome our obsession with food is if we *want* to change. We can listen to others tell us we need to lose weight, to be more healthy, or stop our obsession, but until we can do this on our own terms, we will never succeed.

We use food too often as a cure for our depression, to fill holes, and to self-soothe. The question is why we use food. Where are we missing out in life that makes food is the *best* filler of our needs?

I was filling several holes. First was food deprivation in general. I had dieted so much and beat myself up for enjoying food for so long that I felt I needed to eat as much food again as possible, before the next diet or famine.

I also reached back and saw the direct correlation to control and my childhood. Having someone tell me I was overweight for a sport impacted me so severely, it affected my food choices and my body image. That is why *now* I believe I have the most treasured job in the world. I am able to connect with young, impressionable gymnasts and women and teach them how to love their body, how to search for strength, healing, and nourishment in food, and not use it as punishment or reward. I now know I am helping every young gymnast I touch.

Every clinic I do, every child who listens to me educate them on how to eat foods that will help them get stronger, tighter, and quicker, I am having an impact. My mission now is purely to help the young women who have faced the horrible notion that they are too heavy, fat, and not good enough. I want them to learn that there *ARE* proper foods they can enjoy and that will *HELP* them be awesome. I want to be the educator I never had.

My Mission is to help gymnasts!

Working with parents, educating them on how to fuel correctly for gymnastics

THE FINAL STEPS... *AND THIS IS FROM MY HEART*

AFTER MOVING BACK to America, I quickly jumped back into personal training my clients in Cincinnati, and I also started training gymnasts again. I was well on my way to ending my binge eating, at that point. I would occasionally eat too much, but bingeing was finished. I was also starting to work with gymnasts and women who also suffered from binge eating issues. I felt their pain and shared my story about how I found balance again and overcame the dreaded addictions to food, obsessive dieting, and exercising.

Don't get me wrong, I struggled a lot in the beginning to overcome my addiction to foods. I feared that, one day, I would go back to my old ways. I was afraid of getting fat again. I feared depression, losing my business...

And I still struggled with body image issues. The bingeing did a number on my body. I had a lot of stretch marks and cellulite, and my skin didn't seem to be bouncing back as it once did. I worried that all of the damage I did by yo-yoing up and down thirty pounds time after time had created permanent damage to my body. That was what I was experiencing. But now, I was at peace with it, because my perspective on life changed from being all about me to all about my family.

Of course, the drastic weight change had caused dimples, stretch marks, and some hanging skin. However, over time, they started to go away as I reintroduced healthy fats, greens, and legumes, and went on more of a plant-based diet. Initially, I was really worried about this, but then I started studying functional foods and how they could heal and repair the body.

Functional foods are foods that have added health benefits to them. They fight free radicals, viruses, and fungus; they enhance metabolic rates, and aid in joint, muscle, and skin repair. They help our hearts, our brains, and our skin (the biggest organ in our bodies). When I started looking at food as medicine, things really clicked.

I knew that I had to return to functional foods to help with my skin and digestion, so I studied these in depth. I started to research foods that would help me live longer and be stronger.

I decided to go back to school and learn more about nutrition. I upgraded my sports nutrition certification to a college-accredited program. In the process, I began to share these ideas with my clients, gymnasts, and other people struggling with weight issues and other debilitating diseases.

I started to experiment with spices, different veggies, and fruits, creating healthy dishes with garlic, onions, peppers, different fats like olive and coconut oil, and seeds, lots of seeds and grains—all foods I thought I could never enjoy again!

I also included bread, dark chocolate, quinoa, and butter into my diet, foods I would never have allowed myself to eat while restricting, the very foods I would binge on because they were forbidden.

If you look in my cupboard now, you will find whole grains, nuts, oils, nut butters, and *carbs*! In my fridge, you will find whole butter, cream, eggs, and berries, loads of fruit and veggies, fish, and lots of greens.

These are the foods that make me look younger, feel better, and live leaner! They also made me fertile! I was able to get pregnant naturally at thirty-nine and forty-one. I finally found the right combination of all these foods, the one that was best me.

Now, I'm traveling the country and sharing my online programs, helping to create meal plans, and teaching how to put these balanced food groups together to get your best body ever. Food is medicine, food is fuel, and food is amazing, if eaten in the right combinations.

I believe in what I'm doing now, because I'm living it. I am in the best mental and physical shape *together* at the same time that I have ever been.

If I can do this after all I have been through, then I believe so can everyone else! I have no doubt that binge eating *can* be overcome, but everyone has their own path. It really depends on how bad you want it. If you are ready to take the steps to overcome your addiction, the time is now... "Even the longest journey begins with a single step."

YOUR ANSWERS

HOW BAD DO YOU WANT IT???

ONLY *YOU* CAN FIND the answer to that question. However, I can give you clues and hope that you will and can overcome this terrible problem.

This was my personal formula. Yours will be different, but these were the steps I took:

I allowed myself to "get fat."

➢ I dug deep, read, researched, and listened to others to find balance; a lot of it was finding peace within me.

➢ I allowed myself to stop dieting by eating a balance of foods.

➢ I married a Frenchman and ate like the French.

➢ I realized over time who I was, what I

wanted, and that what I wanted to present to the world wasn't a binge eater. It was *ME*!

ALSO.....

> I let go of the low-fat diet.

> I let go of the low-carb diet.

> I let go of doing cardio every day for three hours or more.

> I let go of restrictive eating.

> I gave myself freedom.

> I decided who I wanted to be for my family and my children, really looking at myself closely.

> I decided I wanted to *live* and be a role model for young women and others who have struggled.

> I had children and realized, "It's not all about me!"

And with this I stopped bingeing, I had two babies, regained confidence, and I am now teaching others how to overcome eating obsessions and eat a balanced array of foods and treats, too!

AND SO, WHAT IS YOUR CALL TO ACTION?

Right now, you may be reading this and saying, "I can't do it." Or, "This may have worked for her, but it can't for me. I'm addicted and I love to eat..."

I KNOW!

I WAS THERE!

I know that feeling of thinking about food every waking moment....

But there IS more to life than food. Right now you may be so addicted and so deep that you feel it is hopeless, that you are destined for a life of misery... Perhaps you aren't bingeing on food but on alcohol, drugs, sex, spending money, or hoarding. Everyone has their own way of dealing with stress, pain, and struggle.

Each of you will have your own path in this journey of overcoming, but know this: I understand you! That is why now I work with yo-yo dieters, binge eaters, ex-athletes, and gymnasts who struggle to eat balanced, clean meals due to the stress of their sport or past experiences. I want to help every person I can who has struggled with these issues. I want to give hope and inspiration and say, "It can be done! I have done it! You can, too."

Right now, if you are struggling with food addiction, you have two choices. You can continue on the same path and hope that, one day, all will be better and you will stop obsessing over food. You will continue to be in the same rut you are in or have always been, hoping one day the magic pill or answer will arise...

Or you can take massive action and take steps to overcome your binge eating by ending the dieting cycle and forbidden food game, by trying new foods, and allowing yourself to choose who you want to be and searching for higher meaning in life than food. Consider self-study or reaching out to a trainer or nutritionist who will work with you to find balance and happiness and help to overcome your eating problem.

What will be your formula to end the food addiction you are facing? One thing is for sure: nothing will change if you continue on your current path.

I am available to help anyone structure a meal plan that they can live with. I can help guide those struggling with the right direction, listen, and give needed support. The amazing thing about the Internet is that I am able to touch thousands of people through my online programs, which include motivation, inspiration, recipes, and meal plans. My plans incorporate the balance needed to overcome addictive eating. I also create energizing meal plans for gymnasts with the right combination and balance of food groups.

My work now carries over into gymnastics academies all over the world. I come into gyms with my fitness and nutrition camps and help coaches and gymnasts get educated on processed foods and on foods that help athletes excel without feeling restricted or like they are on a diet. Education is so crucial. Once we allow ourselves to eat all food groups in a balanced and moderate way, extremes can dissipate.

Right now the culture of USA Gymnastics is in the process of changing its leadership and moving toward a positive and healthy experience for children. I want to contribute and be part of that healthy movement, especially with respect to a positive self-image in such a demanding sport.

So, whether you are a gymnast, a former athlete, a competitor, a mom, a dad, or a person with food addiction, I am giving you a call to action! Today is the day. If you know someone who is struggling with finding balance, or if you yourself are struggling, *please*, take action and turn your life around. Make it one where you feel comfortable again in your own skin. Where you can enjoy pizza and chocolate in moderation and still feel great in a bathing suit. So you can look attractive to your mate or wear that dress you want to wear! What are you waiting for? I did it, and if I can, so can you!

Are you ready to change?

BETSY MCNALLY

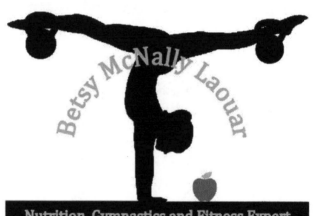

ACKNOWLEDGMENTS

I WOULD BE REMISS not to thank all of the people who have influenced my book, both good and bad.

My parents, who have always supported me, James and Carolyn McNally. My husband, Mess, who is my biggest fan and father to my amazing children. My children, Lenny and Ayden, who are reason for my living.

My good friends, who got me through the dark years of my bingeing and self-destruction, specifically Mandy Zaransky-Hurst. My gymnastics coaches, who helped me directly and indirectly become the person I am today. Amelia Hundley, an Elite gymnast I trained one-on-one for several years, who showed me what a fighter can do.

Molly Shawen-Kollman, who has always supported and believed in my mission. Mary Lee Tracy, renowned coach at Cincinnati Gymnastics, who launched me back into the world of gymnastics. Dr. Alison Arnold, for all her help, and who I am currently working with in our Tight Mind Tight Body Bootcamps to help gymnasts all over the world.

And all of my clients, gymnasts, parents, and coaches, who give me daily inspiration to educate, help, and inspire young women around the globe.

I say *thank you* for inspiring ME.

ABOUT BETSY

BETSY MCNALLY-LAOUAR is a graduate of Michigan State University with a degree in English Education. She is a certified personal trainer under the NSCA and holds several Sports Nutrition Certifications, including one from Chicago State University. She works primarily with gymnasts, from little-level ones to Olympians, in nutrition and fitness. She was a level-ten gymnast at Queen City Gymnastics and a coach at Cincinnati Gymnastics.

She is a professional fitness competitor in the IFBB and a recovered binge eater. She is an author, mother, wife, and friend to many clients around the world whom she has helped in the areas of fitness, nutrition, and wellness.

She currently travels the country doing her nutrition and fitness camps for gymnasts, and she coaches and runs an online nutrition and fitness programs for all types of people.

She is available to create individual training and nutrition plans for you.

Find more about how at: www.BetsyMcnally.com

Reach Betsy at: Coach@BetsyMcnally.com

And check out her programs here:

https://coache16fe5.clickfunnels.com/9-week-challenge-regular

Made in the USA
Columbia, SC
14 April 2020